SIMPLE BLESSINGS

Coloring Book

Scriptures and Inspirations to Color Your World

Art & Design by Karla Dornacher

www.karladornacher.com • www.etsy.com/shop/karladornacher
Karla Dornacher Designs
Vancouver, WA 98664

simple Blessings

scriptures and inspirations to color your world

I love drawing, doodling... and coloring! I always have!
Since I became aware that this art ability was a gift was from God,
it's been my desire to use my art to glorify the Lord... and to be a blessing and encouragement to others.
I am thrilled to be able to combine these two passions within the pages of this coloring book...
sharing my heart... and my art... in a way that will hopefully be inspiring and encouraging to you!

This book is designed for artists of all ages...
especially for the child who lives within all of us... no matter what our age!

You will find that the designs are printed on the front of each page only.
This will allow you to remove them from the book, trim them to size, and drop them
into a standard 8x10 frame for gift giving or for your own pleasure and encouragement.

These designs are perfect for crayons, colored pencils, watercolors, watercolor pencils, and markers.
To help prevent colors from bleeding through the back side of the page,
place a blank sheet of paper or cardstock between the pages when coloring.

I hope these illustrations bring you hours of restful coloring pleasure...
and may God richly bless the creativity of your heart and hands!

With love and God-hugs... Karla

Contents

Whether scripture... or inspired by scripture...
these verses are sure to encourage your heart and lift your spirit!

give thanks with a grateful heart

©Karla Dornacher

Trust in the Lord with all your heart

PROVERBS 3:5

©Karla Dornacher

with God...
all things
are {POSSIBLE}

MARK 10:27

©Karla Dornacher

©Karla Dornacher

You are a shield

You bestow GLORY on me and Lift up my head

around me, O Lord ~ Psalm 3:3

Your blessing is upon Your people

©Karla Dornacher

Grow in grace

©Karla Dornacher

2 Peter 3:18 NIV

REST IN THE LORD

Psalm 37:7

A vessel of God's glory

I'm a little tea pot

Tip me over Lord and pour me out

©Karla Dornacher

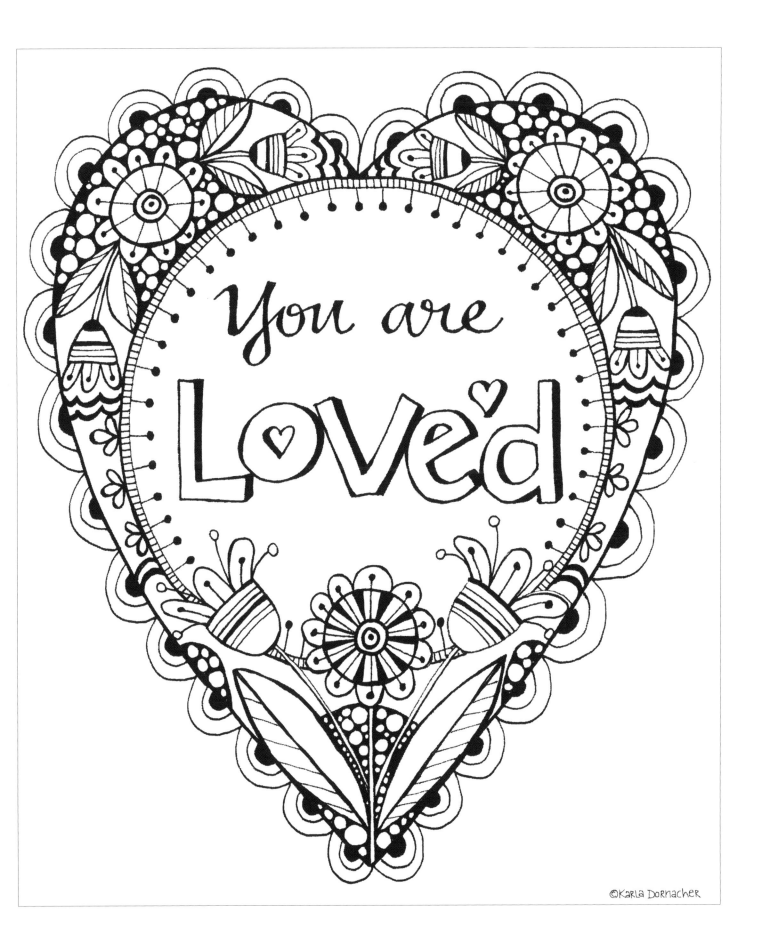

You are Loved

©Karla Dornacher

Plant kindness gather love

©Karla Dornacher

your Grace is sufficient for me

2 Cor 12:9

©Karla Dornacher

©Karla Dornacher

It is better to get wisdom than gold.

©Karla Dornacher
Proverbs 16:16

the JOY of the Lord is my strength

27046973R00031